Sometimes I'm Jealous

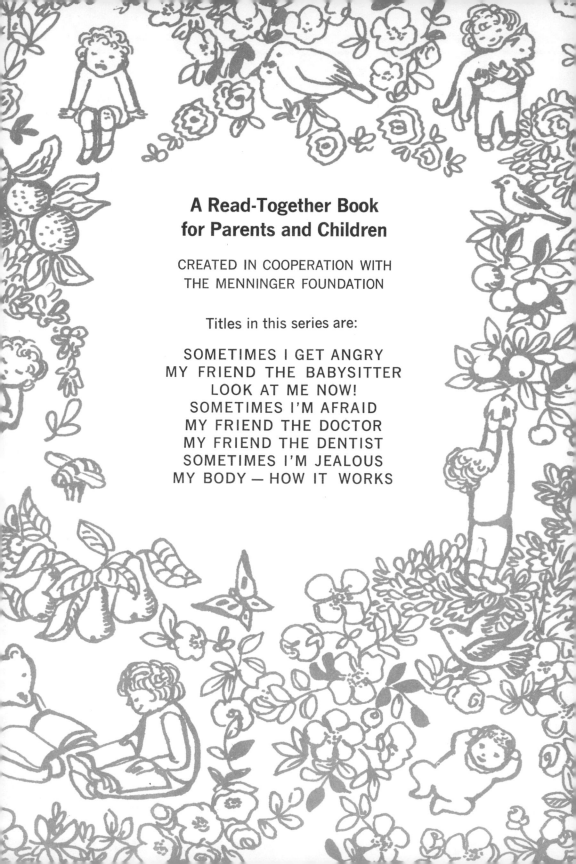

**A Read-Together Book
for Parents and Children**

CREATED IN COOPERATION WITH
THE MENNINGER FOUNDATION

Titles in this series are:

SOMETIMES I GET ANGRY
MY FRIEND THE BABYSITTER
LOOK AT ME NOW!
SOMETIMES I'M AFRAID
MY FRIEND THE DOCTOR
MY FRIEND THE DENTIST
SOMETIMES I'M JEALOUS
MY BODY — HOW IT WORKS

A Read-Together Book
for Parents and Children

CREATED IN COOPERATION WITH
THE MENNINGER FOUNDATION

The Dorothy Wright Treatment and Endowment Fund
defrays a part of the care and treatment cost at the
Children's Division of The Menninger Clinic,
Box 829, Southard Place, Topeka, Kansas 66601.
Part of the income from the sale
of this book goes to that fund.

Sometimes I'm Jealous

by
JANE WERNER WATSON

ROBERT E. SWITZER, M.D.
Director of the Children's Division
The Menninger Clinic

J. COTTER HIRSCHBERG, M.D.
Associate Director of the Children's Division
The Menninger Clinic

Illustrated by
HILDE HOFFMANN

 GOLDEN PRESS • NEW YORK
WESTERN PUBLISHING COMPANY, INC.
Racine, Wisconsin

Library of Congress Catalog Card Number: 77-181431

Copyright © 1972 by Western Publishing Company, Inc.
Printed in the U.S.A.

GOLDEN® and GOLDEN PRESS® are trademarks
of Western Publishing Company, Inc.

NOTE TO PARENTS

Ideally each newborn child is a wanted baby and is for some time made the center of his small world. Until he is about three or four months old, the baby is not really aware of the difference between himself and his world. When he does become conscious of Mother as a separate person, he feels that she exists just for him. By seven months, he is aware not only of Mother and her special importance to him but of other people as well; he becomes anxious in the presence of unfamiliar persons. Mother's comforting usually reassures him that all is well around him and that he can still feel in control.

Inevitably though, Baby experiences the disappointing realization of not being in complete control of his world. He feels hungry, and Mother doesn't always produce food instantly. He wakens, and she is not always in view. He wants to be held close and Mother isn't there to pick him up. He wets and has to wait awhile for dry clothing.

Gradually Baby learns that even though he may have to wait for what he wants, he can count on Mother. He learns that Daddy too can be depended on to respond to his needs. He also learns that Daddy's love and sharing of activities with Mother make her happy, and Baby feels her happiness.

As the toddler's development continues, his world expands, but he continues to see himself as its center, with everything circling around him and belonging to him. By the time he is walking and using words, though, he has learned he can not always have things his way, that other children—and grown-ups—have wishes as strong as his. He has learned that some experiences are painful and make him cry. These are important lessons to learn. If the child comes to them with a basic trust carried over from the early baby months when he was the center of his secure little world, he will learn the lessons and not be defeated by them. He will retain his sense of security.

The child comes to know that some things he does Mother likes. Other things irritate or anger her. He knows that even when she is angry, she still loves him, but he learns to value doing things that she likes and having her praise him. He still thinks of himself before thinking of others, so he sometimes does things Mother doesn't like.

The small child resents anything—such as competition with other children—that diminishes his importance. Not surprisingly then, learning that Mother is going to have a new baby makes him feel that he is being displaced. He hears talk about the new baby; much is made of getting ready for it. As Mother is now more than usually concerned about herself and her health, and Daddy is more concerned about Mother, the child tends to feel left out.

Letting him take part in preparations and share in the plans lessen this jealousy, and the child may even pretend that Mother is having the baby just for him to play with. The facts remain though: Mother will be going away to give birth to the new baby; when they return, the new baby will take time, love and attention. This will mean a great change in the small child's self-centered world.

Daddy can play a strong part in helping the child to accept the change happily by making it clear to the worried youngster that his love is warm and unchanged. When symptoms of jealousy—overt resentment of the baby or regression to infantile patterns—appear, as they may, they should be met with affectionate reassurance. With thoughtful advance preparation by his parents and lots of love along the way, the child will come through this crisis of growth secure enough of his own place so that he can help the new baby to enjoy being the center of its small world just as he once was—and no longer needs to be.

Robert E. Switzer, M.D.
Director of Children's Division
THE MENNINGER CLINIC

J. Cotter Hirschberg, M.D.
Associate Director of Children's Division
THE MENNINGER CLINIC

Do you know what I like?
I like having my own way.
I like getting what I want,
right now,
not having to wait my turn.
I like having Mother and Daddy
pay attention to me—
nobody else, just me!

I guess when I was a baby
I got my way most of the time.
I can't really remember
long ago when I was a baby,
but I guess then
I was really the center of things.

Mother was always there
to hold me
and give me what I wanted.
When I was hungry, she fed me.
When I was full, she burped me.
When I was wet or had a b.m.,
she changed my diaper.

If I felt lonesome, I cried.
Then somebody held me
and I felt better.

If I wanted something,
I grabbed for it.
I didn't think
about anyone but me.

Later I learned that some things
I did made Mother and Daddy
unhappy with me.
When they were unhappy
they seemed further away,
and I felt troubled.

I learned that other things I did
made them happy—
things like learning to eat new foods
and giving up the bottle,
things like waiting to go
to the bathroom to potty and b.m.
It was fun to be able to do things
that made them happy.
Then they seemed warm and close,
and I felt happy too.

Sometimes another child came to play.
The other child wanted to be
the center of things too.
He wanted the toys
when he wanted them,
without waiting his turn.
I wanted them too!
If he fell down and cried,
Mother held him
to make him feel better.
I felt left out and hurt.
I felt jealous.
But that was just once in a while.

Then Mother and Daddy told me
we were going to have
a new baby at our house.
At first I didn't know
what they meant.
I was the new baby
at our house.
I thought it would
always be that way.
Then I thought
they were getting the baby
to be a plaything for me.
I thought Mother and I
would take care of it together.
Mother and I would still
be together all the time.
I would still be the center of things.

But even before the baby came,

things began to be different.

Mother didn't feel good sometimes.

She didn't feel like playing

with me then.

She got cross and tired.

Daddy said she was not her usual self.

He did things for her

and sometimes forgot about me.

Mother and Daddy bought lots of things
for the new baby.
Some were toys I wanted to play with.
They didn't let me.
They brought the crib I slept in
when I was a baby
down from the attic.
They fixed up my baby room
for the new baby.

I was glad I was getting big
and wasn't a baby any more.
Mother and Daddy were glad too.
But I wasn't all glad.
I wasn't in the center any more.
I felt jealous.

All this time
Mother's tummy was getting bigger
because the new baby
was growing inside her.
I could tell it was there
because Mother let me feel her tummy
when the baby moved and kicked.
Daddy was pleased
about the new baby coming.
He had helped Mother start it.
But I wanted him to be pleased with me.

I wondered how the new baby
would get out of Mother's tummy.
Mother said the baby would come out
through a special opening
between her legs.
I was born that way too.
Mother said she would go
to the hospital to have the new baby.
She said mothers go to the hospital
to have new babies
so the doctors can help
when the baby is ready to be born.

I know about the hospital.
I said I'd come to see her there.
Mother said only grown-ups can visit
in the part where the new babies are.
I didn't like that.
I didn't like her going away
and my not being able to visit her.
I felt left out.
I felt jealous.

Sometimes I wished there was no new baby.
I wished things could be
like they had been.
I wanted to be the center of things again.
Daddy said someone nice
would stay with me
when he took Mother to the hospital.
He said it would be someone I knew
like my babysitter or my grandma.
But I still didn't like it.
I felt sad and mad.

One day Mother said,
"Please come and help me
pack a bag for the hospital.
I don't know just when this baby
will be ready to come.
I don't know just when
I will have to go."
I helped her pack.
I put in one of my stuffed animals
to keep her company.
She said she would miss me.

Then the time came.

The baby was ready to come.

Mother and Daddy went to the hospital.

I cried because I felt left out.

I knew where Mother was, and why,

but I wanted her home with me.

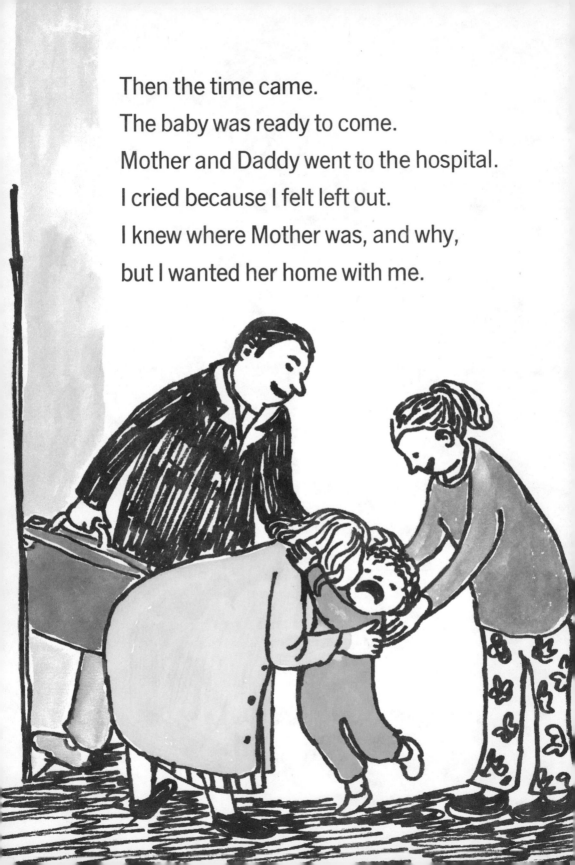

Then the telephone rang.

It was for me.

It was Daddy calling

to tell me the baby was born.

He said Mother and the baby were fine.

They were taking a nap.

Later Daddy drove me by the hospital.
He showed me Mother's window.
He said, "Having this new baby
in the family
will be a change for us all.
I know you are not sure
how you feel about it right now.
But we have enough love
to give some to the new baby
without any less for you."

The day after the baby was born,
Mother talked to me on the phone.
"I love you," she said.
"I miss you, but I have your toy
right in my room, and it keeps me company.
I will bring it back
when the new baby and I come home.
Thank you for helping Daddy
get ready for us."
I felt better when I talked
to Mother and Daddy,
but the days Mother was away
seemed a long time.
Sometimes I felt jealous.

Then they came home.

I was so happy to see Mother.

I wanted to see the baby too.

It really wasn't much.

Mostly it was a bundle of baby clothes.

It didn't look like anybody.

It couldn't talk or do anything

but eat and sleep and fill its diapers.

When it cried, Mother came

to feed it or change it or hold it.

People came to see the new baby.

They brought presents for it.

All they talked about was that baby.

Some of them didn't even see me.

The new baby was the center

of everything, it seemed.

I felt left out.

I wanted to be noticed too,

so I tried acting like the baby.

It didn't really work, though.

I didn't really want to be a baby again.

I like to talk and walk
and play and learn new things.
New babies can't do any of that.
Daddy and Mother are so pleased
with all I can do.
They say it will be a long time
before the baby can do
all I can do now.
By then, I'll be way ahead of it again.
Mother lets me go outside to play.
The baby can't do that.
I play with other children.
I like that better all the time.
The baby can't do that.
When I come in,
Mother is glad to see me.
When Daddy comes home,
he is glad to see me.

The baby takes a lot of time,
and gets in the way sometimes.
But Mother still loves me.
Daddy still loves me.
And I like the baby too,
now that I know
it hasn't pushed me out
of my place in the family.
I'm still me,
and I'm growing up,
and I like it.